Thirst

Donal O'Connell

"I laugh when I hear that the fish in the water is thirsty:

You do not see that the real is in your home,

And you wander from forest to forest listlessly!

Here is the truth! Go where you will ,

To Benares or to Mathura :

If you do not find your soul,

The world is unreal to you."

Kabir.

"What can be attained is the elimination of privilege. This is really the work before the whole world. In all social lives, there has been one fight in every race and in every country. The difficulty is not that one body of men are naturally more intelligent than another, but whether this body of men, because they have advantage of intelligence, should take away even physical enjoyment from those who do not possess that advantage. The fight is to destroy that privilege."
- *Vivekananda*

"O FRIEND! hope for Him whilst you live, know whilst you live, understand whilst you live: for in life deliverance abides.

If your bonds be not broken whilst living, what hope of deliverance in death? It is but an empty dream, that the soul shall have union with Him because it has passed from the body:

If He is found now, He is found then, If not we do but go to dwell in the City of Death. If you have union now, you shall have it hereafter. Bathe in the truth, know the true Guru, have faith in the true Name! Kabir says: "It is the Spirit of the quest which helps; I am the slave of this Spirit of the quest."

 - Kabir

Table of Contents

<u>Know You Are Equal</u>

Know you are equal

I am speaking to my brothers

This earth is yours

This air is yours

This sky is yours

You're as equal as the birds that fly

As the animals that graze

As the lions that roar their proclamations of

supremacy

Yes my brother

You are the man

Yes you are the gifted one

Listen my brother

Now is the time to step forth.

Who Am I Today?

Who am I today?

Am I the one who lived fulfilled in yesterday?

Or maybe, I am the one who staggered

 And bumped into truths and recognized none,

Or maybe one,-momentarily!

And in that breath, I met my shadow

And forgave me my humanity

As I caressed my scar tissue

With gratitude and affection for the lessons hard

earned.

The drunk that ogled back

 From the pain-free zone of middle distance,

Who shrugged the shoulder and inclined the head

In a knowing familiarity,

I winked at him in the bar mirror,

He rubbed his eye to check.

It could be me says I, says him, to himself maybe.

The music hall echoes in the canyons of the mind

"My old man says follow the band and

Don't dilly dally on the way?"

I lurch on through life and grope within for truth.

—

<u>Going For Water</u>

Sometimes it feels like yesterday

That Mama clanked the galvanized bucket,

So I sprang to answer the summons.

I preferred the enamel bucket,

Even that it was bigger and heavier

'Cause it had a wooden grip that didn't cut into my
fingers.

It was a fair haul to that well.

Yet water was needed and someone

Had to go 'cause the hungry child needed his bottle,

And your father wanted his tea when he'd wake up.

Anyway –'twas great to be out.

The birds were up and rabbits were still playing

In the shimmery grass,

While the silvery cobwebs glistened in the morning
sunlight.

Your breath puffed out in front of you for company.

You were JJ Barry, Tommy Doyle, Pat Stakelum,

A definite hero to be out so early and all alone

As you ran for a while to stay warm.

Snowdrops and crocuses were under the big trees

And primroses were starting to flash on the banks.

Old dead leaves were crunchy underfoot,

Rocks were slippery and ice not to be trusted.

The cuckooing comfort sound of pigeons in the
branches overhead,

Active in the shadows of the dappled light

Proclaimed an over ground dimension of life and
strife,

An excitement for future exploration and discovery.

Running by the swollen rushing river

That overflowed the banks in spots,

And left green and brown rushes and grass

Standing clear like small islands

On a frozen white and flaky landscape that crunched
in crackling sound.

A little boy that was me imagined

And visualized all of Russia to be like this.

My mother had a pair of Russian boots and

I was wearing them this morning with
My feet nice and cozy while breaking ice
Even that they flopped as I ran,
They were way beyond the bare feet flying
In case of frozen stuck to the iced cobbled stone,
Now that was sore!

Memory of past pain endured, enhanced the gratitude
And embraced the improved present
And invited my spirit to soar like the midday lark
Over a sunlit heat hazed cornfield.
On high I overlooked and over saw
And dawdled in my day dreams.
Alone like this I could ponder and meander
Through the minefields forbidden me by the black
cloth punishers,
Their canes and leathers,
Their dour derisive directions,
Were diminishing and distorted
And I could be for one brief moment me,
Breathing full without fear in the present tense.

Skirting the top edge of the black lake,

A water hen darted across the drowning leaves,

Alerting the diving otters to my presence.

They glanced my way almost in recognition and
continued in their routines.

Onward I sped across the slippery, sleeper bridge

A short cut for able adults.

To clear the mill race flow,

An eight foot span of deep water rushing.

One breath in, one breath out.

You made it again! and continued.

Forbidden fruit was tasty then,

Punishable with a heavy thrashing,

So the evasion was one up on adults

Who were always too busy to explain what the danger
really was.

"Pain was normal every day,

You had to pay for all your play, that was the way"

Inside the door was adult domain,

Dominated by destructive derision

That let you know your place was to be seen and not heard,

So to survive you suppressed

And waited for liberation.

The door opened and you ran and ran and ran for revolution,

Towards liberty, equality, fraternity,

And the dogs ran with you.

They were loyal and they loved unconditionally,

And they showed it by touch and eye contact.

Having survived the danger of crossing the slippery railway sleeper,

The feeling of renewal that one gets after being saved,

An on-rush of feelings and emotions coursed through me

In appreciation of having conquered fear once again

The adrenalin was as sweet as ice cream or bananas,

These were two of the post war novelties that were recent arrivals in rural Ireland.

I hurried with my bucket,

Its handle gripped tight against its side

To avoid any noise or sound of clanking.

Along the bank a mallard was nesting,

Not much of a nest –mind you –

A few twigs and some rushes interlaced

And I knew it would not be long before the duck egg

blues would be visible.

The wind was at my back,

So two snipe rose up nearly in my face before veering

off in flashing flight,

Leaving me gulping in excitement and startlement.

As I neared the bridge up close to the creamery

Where there were a lot of bulrushes,

A swan stretching out his neck was warning me to

keep my distance, and I did.

Last year I got a crack of a wing on the bare leg,

And the memory still stung.

They were nesting there again.

I made the bridge and climbed through the stile,

One step up on a slippery stone platform,

And oh! I knew it wasn't my morning for "everything
going my way."
The white frost mold on the pump handle,
And nearly an inch thick of ice on the trough,
Spelled struggle for a young lad short in stature.

Nevertheless, the little fellow needed his bottle,
And the auld fellow wanted his tea.
'Twas up to me.

The bucket got dented trying to break the ice
For you had to have water from the trough,
To prime the pump to work the pump.
A rock I got and hopped it twice, to crack the ice.
It splintered eventually and I got the bucket half full
To pour into the pump head and make the handle pull
The lovely fresh clean water from down below.
I pumped some strokes and prayed that I wouldn't
have to prime again and again.

Eventually I felt it grip, the water gushed,
And power and pleasure rushed through me in a thrill,

For trough and bucket would have their fill.

Success was mine today.

I'd get this home to mam

And have my toasted "Cashel Grinder*" with the tea,

Do my lessons and learn my table before going of to school.

The dogs and the little fellow would be there when I came home.

A great life!

If you didn't weaken.

Where's me hurley? I have to go!

*a colloquial name for a turnover loaf of bread made in Cashel, Co. Tipperary.

A Pumped Wheelbarrow

Well its the luxury of a pumped wheelbarrow

That makes my day seem bright.

Those heavy loads

Where all is uphill

Can be a two step

Squeaky music and the light.

Now shoveling hard

Can be a bummer,

Like digging drains

In cold wind and rain,

But I got me a pumped wheelbarrow,

And the sun will shine again.

18th November '87

Am I Lonely?

To search for work in polluted air,
In a rambling city that's dark and bare
Of the gentle nonchalance
And devil may care
Of people at their ease.
I'm slowly dying, in this
Briefcase land,
Where drawn faces,
Travel underground,
And machinery noise,
Is the constant sound.
I long to hear the chirp of birds
Not skuttering pigeons
In search of junk.
Oh! to gaze upon a smiling face.

London, 1984

18

A Requiem

The ding ding and clack clack

Of the tram gliding by downstairs

Is soothing to me the rural interloper

Returning to the Nice of my youth.

The tainted bog Ireland suck of the

Nineties and noughties has drained

My passionate patriotism

And embarrassed my integrity.

Looking about me here remembering,

The street life, the Cafe bar and

Sidewalk banter of the early sixties

The thirty franc "dames du nuit" now

Up marketed by inflation yet-

Retaining their camaraderie and sense of humor

Alluring lust in the Cote d'Azur.

Museums and Galleries are mostly free

In memory of la Liberty, Equality, Fraternity,

"C'est vraie ici "unlike

The pathetic Rip off Republic Irlandaise

Of gobshite strokers we have become

Amidst the diarrhea of the "Tiger"

Saints and Scholars along time ago

Brought learning to Britain and to and fro

We Irish learned to come and go

Through out Europe with respect

And with respect its now only

Bawdy bowsies

With Irish Pub above the door

A dirty toilet and urine floor

I am sad that we have sunk so low

And could not sober up

To mature and grow.

God we had potential !

Is it too late for reinvention?

Cosy I am

Cosy I am inside my skin today

Drinking café con leche in Place de la Libertad

Under a parasol in hot noonday sunshine.

Pedestrians are beehive busy before siesta time

Moroccan sunglass sellers are on parade

Skiving and diving 'tis a part of their trade

I love having time to relax and take stock

Timing out to unwind, allowing brain to unlock

And then a blonde with some bottom

Has swished past my chair

Hair tresses still flouncing

Perfuming the air

Double kissing the waiter

Her café comes pronto

He shapes like Lone Ranger

And regards her as Tonto

Fanore Strand

Four necklace strings of white billowed foam

Reach forward to embrace my breath of vision.

Shifting shells, sand and stones with swishing sounds

The seashore shines in shimmering shuddering shifts

And shunts its mass with sure strength swell

Like a muscle flex response from moon.

To day I feel right small on this Atlantic shelf

With Burren mountains at my back,

Flesh pink orchids and gentians blue are fading too

Midsummer approaches heralds the turn of tiding time

And remind me that the spring has come and gone .

Oh! white faced people of bucket and spade

Oh! weekend frolickers from colour TV.

Oh! yellow topped, swarthy swathed,

Swelled bosomed middle aged greys,

Please laugh this year ,we need to hear,

The tinkling remembrance of a far off bell

That rang out with a thrill,

To say to all that once upon a time,

You too were young!

Just like I feel here today.

Opa in der Bahnhof

Opa in der Bahnhof long ago-

Steam trains hissed their impatience

To down nach ein grosses and glow

With further apprehension on one hand

And promptings to continue and explore on the other.

The grizzled face of the old guy

With bemused wrinkle laugh lines round the eyes

Who spoke of Goethe and Dostoyevsky of Yates and
Oscar Wilde

And how we were all in jail

Self imprisoned with church boundaries

And by rules we can't obey.

Comings and goings all change the only constant

Now you have it and now you don't.

Oblivion beckons from many quarters

Last night's shadowy memories are unsettling

They urge one to plunge headlong and escape

Run from the phantoms deny their existence.

Faces, faces, faces, flash, flash, flash, each indelible

With eyes of intelligence registering memory

They have seen they have known secrets.

Hide, hide the hideous the unsavoury the unsettling
The liver twisting mind screeching shameful sham.
Shuffling shifting sliding slithering slippery sickness
Of selfish self-loathing and self indulgence onwards
Onwards to the confessional where the power seeker
Sits in waiting for, for, for?-for-nic-ation to thrust
deeper
Into the bowels, the depths where sin and shame and
guilt began
Where fear was baptized and given form to rule
To rule innocence with imperial censure and
unceasing remonstration.

The kingdom? Where oh! Where the domain of king?
Where does freedom reign?
In heaven, the kingdom lives within, the place or state
where the blessed see and enjoy.
Liberty-equality-fraternity.-the abolition of privilege
for the few and the granting of privilege to the masses
is love, is love,amamous those of us who are free.

Free – Freedom-free domain- where liberty dominates
where censure is exiled and restriction is absent
eruption ensues volcanic in temperament like a lanced
boil from those who knew only incarceration-
licentious leanings surface after years of tethering and
balance is precarious to say the least yet laughter and
good fellowship can lead gently and guide towards
fair play.
Opa your white moustache with frothy flecks still
bristle today in memory
The craggy face bemused by youth's enthusiasm and
gullible generosity gently rocks
And nods affirmatives to the remaining remnants of
cathartic cynicism.

A vivid flashback to a railway bar in Wiesbaden,
Germany.1964

Phyllis Gallagher, Leicester Square

Phyllis Gallagher, alone with your sherry in Leicester

Square,

I feel such kinship with you there.

The rumbling trains that came and went,

The people passing did not want to know

Of your suffering Douglas,

Your tale of woe.

You sat so frail with your doctor's slip,

A ticket to God knows what chemicals,

And some head shrinker's trip.

Oblivion's warmth in a hospital bed,

Believing that heaven is after your dead.

Your hands were warm,

Your eyes were kind,

Your gray hairs parted and freshly combed,

Your plastic bag was your traveling home,

Shivering, shuddering, from feeling alone,

Forgotten by God and cut off to roam.

Tonight I wonder where will be your bed?

London, 1984

Neighbours Gone Bye

I am thinking about you Pete & Annie

Great neighbours I had over

A score years ago.

After your stroke Pete,

With your speech all awry

And four years stuttering and

Not able to say what you

Wanted to say

We met out one day.

In Greene's by the quay

We drank malt whiskey

Till teatime.

That whiskey was like oil on

Troubled water and enabled

Me to hear at slow pace

And interpret for sure your

Words in their jumble tongue

Twisted fashion that were in a maze

But like the cure the whiskey worked.

You clutched my arm,

You refused to let go,

You had found an interpreter

Who could at last deliver

What had been pent up within you

For the last four years.

We set off on the rounds of the town

Some people had to be put right,

Insignificant it was to most of them

But important it was to you Pete.

So some looked at me strongly for

Having so deeply imbibed,

Their impatience barley and grudgingly

Concealed, as I explained Pete's mission.

We straightened some accounts and

Cleared debts with a deoch,

Entered a tavern to see Mrs T

Over messages not delivered

To his sister Annie, that he

Had paid for some years before

And told her that he would not again

Darken her door.

He was soft and gentle with the clearest

Bluest eyes that looked out

With an innocence devoid of all guise.

He would dabble in fun and go

Into riddles and laugh like a

Child when he would stumble

The listener –"What's the half of two

And two"? And after ten minutes of

Teasing –he would shout with glee!

Three!!!.

"What's the first thing a baby does

After been born"??

Many minutes of waiting, then a

Howl of bold laughter after all the failures

Of listeners –"Makes way for another one"

Call a round.

You came home one night Pete

Some what sozzeled lit a

"Gold Flake "and dreamt

Your way further back to mother

And father and those gone before.

The gas bottle exploded,

Blew out the door and
Fanned a funeral pyre for
Your last remains.

My friend Annie I can see you true
In your laced up brogeens
And your smock of blue
Outside your half door.
Dearest Annie you smoked your
Dudeen pipe and recited tales
Of raw ribaldry in Cappamore.
Back when a priest would stamp on
Glee, crush with venom a happy ceili
And seek recruitment for a laundry
Called Magdalena.
Gathering bearts of hazel
For firewood, you boiled
Clothes and scrubbed floors,
You cooked meals for ungrateful
Begrudgers
You trudged the roads from
House to house brought your

Light that never went out

And left behind a step

To freedom.

Those steps you took dear Annie

Across the mountain

To a dance in Lisdoon

And back home after on a

Donkey at dawn are

Traced in the dreams and

Aspirations of devas who live

And who are still to be born,

Your smiling face still

Shines bright the light of joy

As you clapped in time to

Fiddle music from the McGuire Brothers.

The fire in the hearth blazed high

As Dolores K sang "Teddy O Neill"

Backed by Jackie D and Garry O B

'Twas like veils over visions too

Good to be seen-while little

Esther "God rest her" and Anna

Danced fairy reels till dawn.

Those rhythms on the cottage floor

Still ghost the house and forever

More will be part of the memory

Of Cappamore.

A goat was milked that morning

To white the tea and grace the porridge,

Hot cinders were shook off from an old black

Pot oven –a hot soda cake dispensed and devoured

By musicians and dancers.

Your place by the fire,

Shone out towards the stranger

To come in from the door

They were welcome within here

Of that she was sure.

Annie Annie there are not very many

Who grace this earth any more

As the likes of yourself and Pete

Who someday I'll meet, when my

Chores are ore and we will dance

Again like we did in Cappamore.

Till then a gra "Beidh Eireann go Brea"

In a shuil ar bun na sleibhte.

<u>Moving On</u>

There I was sitting on my rucksack
At the crossroads
Facing the sun with my eyes closed,
While the light flickered and danced
Inside my eyelids.
The feeling was good as I listened
To the humming buzz from the vegetation
And surrounding countryside.
The smells from red dust, dried cow dung,
Urine and eucalyptus blended a comfort blanket
Of perfect perfumed security about me –
I was at home in this foreign country
The Latin languages rolled sonorously round
My eardrums gradually decoding the gist
Of the peoples conversation who were gathering
For expectant transport.
With my eyes still closed I pondered
On my current situation,
I was at a turning point – it was time to move on,

Whatever direction this bus was heading

That's where I was going.

The excitement was building within me,

Was it towards a city?

Or was it deeper into the countryside?

I quelled the gathering butterflies in my stomach

With a sincere prayer for acceptance of whatever

This Higher Power's will .for me was

I had ceased running and was in the process

Of embracing freedom –

Yes freedom, with all it's uncertainties!

In a city I would probably rise

To the top of the dung heap, in obduraty.

In the countryside I might realize

The value of manure and experience.

August ' 07

<u>Turning Point Moments</u>

When I was about ten years old,

My grand uncle Pat was ploughing with two horses up above

In Sadliers field beside the Dublin to Cork line near the

Railway bridge in Thurles town.

Uncle Pat stood me before him,

Placed my two hands on the plough's handles

And then covered them with his own two massive paws.

Instructing me to always keep a keen eye as to where

I was walking so as not to stumble, and to constantly

Review the horizontal ridge and furrow.

Then "how, how"and away we went to the accompaniment of

A wonderful sheeing sound being regularly

Punctuated by the grumbling sound of rocks being

Uprooted while the sod was sheared, sliced,

And neatly turned over on its predecessor,

Ever so evenly like lines on a school copy book.

The feeling of power as the horses responded to
My verbal commands of "how how" and "woo" was
For me majestically awesome, unforgettable,
Thanks Pat.
The next time I encountered similar sounds and
feelings was
Ploughing my own garden in Aughnish,an acre and a
half,
I had by hand dug, weeded, manured with dung and
seaweed,
Hoed and mulched the previous year from a body
weight of
Thirteen and a half stone down to nine stone
becoming fit but fatigued
And then to plough that garden the following spring
With a lovely gentle mare named Moll was near
ecstasy,
Especially knowing the value of each yard in
comparative energy expression
Spike harrowing was the opposite experience to
harrowing it was

Delightful, so delightful in fact that it prompted and propelled

A break in my temperance vow of some years to celebrate

Such a release from hard labour.

That horse was hugged with joy, gratitude and affection.

Moll my pet you were strong loyal and dutiful thank you.

The next nearing that sound and experience was greeing ,grating,greshing,

As I ploughed the red clay dusty gravely fertile land with

Two cows in Montes dos Cairos near Aljezur in southern Portugal.

My stubble faced wine loving tutor Antonio and his adoring cooing

Cackling, good humoured wife Marguerita, proud and noble,

Land loving people, who shared without stint their knowledge,

Their lore and culture, two professors of
Mediterranean Horticulture.
Obrigado!

And now here I am stumbling again with more than
Three score years and ten and my own Margueriata
To encourage and help me to weed in a garden near
gone to seed,
Less ambitious it is today, as children are fed and
gone away,
And some day soon it will be my time to go and play
and join the clay.
And then I will soar with the avian travellers and
swallow my way
South for more sunshine.

My Cousin Jimmy

She brought back meadow sweet from Tipperary,

Back from the Horse and Jockey-

From where! –Jimmy's gone!

The heavy sweet scent fills the kitchen

With his absence-

Gone his devilment chuckle!

Three new motors all bundled in a fortnight's forays,

With two Saville Row tailored crumpled suits

And the handmade brown boots

All cattle skutter stained, damp and mouldy blue

hairy

In the car boot, with the everstart naggin, in one of

the pockets.

Ah! Jimmy we played hurling on the lawn

At the crack of dawn,

Before going to Rinanna,

To pick up the uncle yank priests

Returning from Texas.

And not to forget

With your pal Maher in the car,

You captured Brett the county councillor,

To make sure the poor woman got a home.

Now here I am eating Cashel Grinders toasted with

creamery butter.

As I remember you in Ardmayle,

As you layed low, after the boys

Had bribed Scanlon

They had him perm your hair

While asleep in the barber chair you did snore.

You'd been on it for a while

And on that last mile,

You came to our house to rest and recover

And discuss the predicament, with your godmother,

My mother, who always shook her head in

disapproval

And then she'd smile a fine long loving smile

Nod the head a few more times and let you be.

With a sense of humour and a bit of devilment,

You faced all fear and always dared!.

Your chuckle woke me from my sleep

As no other being before or since,

Had ever uttered or stuttered

In such muffled laughter-

Irrerepressible you always were

Where no boundary fence could

There contain or come near to tame that you.

We hurled on the lawn at dawn

With the white frost crisping the grass

Before collecting the yank priests in *Rinanna.

Clocking a ton on the straight concrete road

Where the clackyty clack clacks, got faster, and faster

As we laughed and cheered to beat TWA on landing.

Dear Jimmy your likes will be met again

When liberty shines

And restrictions don't abide.

My Laughing Wild Cousin I Miss You. !!!

*Rinanna now known as Shannon Airport

June 2011

My Godmother

My auntie Diana was herself, to say the least.

In her youth a bright blonde bombshell,

Who could dance the whole night through,

Amuse and entertain, lure men without a strain,

While at dawn could break a horse,

In the afternoon complete a course

Of fences, walls, and obstacles,

Collect rosettes and prizes,

And then come home to babysit

Her little man, her nephew and godson, me.

Off to college she went then,

Took a degree in pharmacy,

Came home and took a tumble from a horse.

Three days later she came round

And they say was never quite as sound,

Had lofty airs and graces, was a little off the ground

And only loved the poor.

Hayes' Hotel was her home from home,

Where she stayed for some years,

And she made it her own.

She crossed over the edge, right over to see,

If she could find, the lost piece of mind,

That differed her brain from the inane,

That made her mad, sad, bad, glad,

Introspection, much reflection, and recollection,

Perused and cruised within the bemused cranium

She lived in a car for a while,

Not far from her late mothers, her brother's and her own place.

During part of her day,

She made her way as a bag lady,

Perambulating, contemplating,

Visiting poor people across town.

With a question mark wrinkle frown between the eyebrows,

She wandered, and wandered, and was loved,

Respected and pitied by those who did not know how proud,

She really was of her superior knowledge,

Her physical and spiritual health,

And her wealth within, wherein she dwelt

In close proximity to the Lord she so proclaimed

To be her sole Shepard.

An impatient wasp in the morning,

A humorous butterfly after lunch,

By evening, devotions and benediction time, a serious saint.

We will meet again and hum Slievenamon*,

If I am let in to your department. *Slievenamon -

"The mountain of the women"

Sundown at Kovalam

For so long now I have followed the sun back down
into the ocean.
For so long now I have howled like a lone wolf at the
moon
Always I felt I was me.
Waves crash upon the shore
Spend their fury to be heard no more
Yet each one rolls again and again
Inside my ocean-
Where tinkle bells sift sand and
Trickle sweet devotion.
The necklace lights of fishermen still out on the sea
Carry me to them with empathy
I am lonely for the sight of Thee,
Lean closer, lean closer to home.
My love, my love, you are within.

The Contenders

Cathair na Gaillimhe City of Tribes,

Sidewalk strollers

Downcast eyes,

Shuffling winos will meet your stare,

Why should they care?

They have laid it bare.

Be glazed bloodshot eyes

Stand out opaque

From weathered grizzled

Spud-fed face.

A sway, a clutch upon the arm,

A look of mockery,

A suppressed leer,

This life is short

A day, a year.

Men in their fifties

Who can't come home

They have been in bed

With the Pope of Rome,

Who called them sinner

While taking their pay

With a promise of heaven,

What about To-Day?

Easter 1983

Subway Surfers

Guardian readers normally gray,

Pointed faces intent,

The back bone of a fallen empire.

Commuters nodding to a rocketing plunge,

Dozers awaiting a friendly touch,

Humanity hanging,

Eyes afraid to look,

In case they see themselves

Looking back.

What's in this tension,

That holds them back

From smiling at this mock charade?

Fear rules the underground,

Apart for some few,

Who have naught to lose,

Except their purse.

This tension, boredom

Is an awful curse.

London 1984.

While Wondering Is There Social Welfare

Waiting, waiting, waiting,

Patiently, calmly amidst the babble,

Now Serving 76.

Panes of glass and metal grids,

Between, betwixt, before,

The checks, the double checks,

The red tape mazes,

And obstacle barricades,

Can be cleared, to even say, maybe.

Maybe to day or maybe tomorrow,

Or perhaps next week.

Who knows! except the man next door,

Whose door is always closed.

Now Serving 82,

Just forty four or fourty five to go, plus...

But now position one and two are closed,

Perhaps for lunch? or some tea break?

Let's hope for miracles

With full tum!

And the man is feeling better!
Or more well disposed!
To those who can't afford to munch,
Or pay the gas, or rent, or
The space to put a sleeping bag
Upon a stretch of floor.

Benefit posters around the room,
So many times have been read,
And re-read before.
Don't ask for fear,
It will halt claim
Or cause confusion to delay
Your name to be entered on
A pay slip.

Sit patiently here in plastic chair,
Make yourself at home,
To spend the day,
In doubtful hope you get some pay,
Or a sign that something's stirring.
Still Serving No 84.

Unbidden Bits Of Memories

Bits of memories came back

Of days long gone asunder,

Threads of passion misplaced

And sure 'twas no wonder.

Being hooked to an express

Without a destination,

Clueless of boarding,

Don't ask me which station-

Fueled and driven by a tireless coal stoker,

Who leered and reveled in the blaze,

"Full steam ahead!" was the order,

Plunge headlong through the haze.

The clack, clack and the rumble,

The shushing, the grumble,

Was part of the rhythm

That gave me the ease

To deny this disease of denial

Going away, far away, far away

All the time.

To be reaching blindly for tomorrow,

Oblivious of today,

Held me in consternation!

So to steady, I had to sway

To the drumbeat of a bongo ,

Epistling from the Congo

Where Lumumba got strung up

By the Balubas so they say.

Who to believe among the spinners?

'Twas poor people as always had to pay.

Addled and brain washed,

I stumbled the heaving corridors,

And like one of my most despicable anti-heroes

Cromwell, who was known to have said,

"A man never travels so high as a man

Who doesn't know where he's going"

And on and on I went believing it to be my birthright

to be high.

High, so high that I could not look down

And see the clueless clown I had become.

Those bathroom mirrors did not lie,

They spelt out clear I would shortly die.

Yet the train I choose was traveling faster,

What loomed ahead was dark disaster

Lurching and trundling the corridors of

powerlessness.

The doorbells and knockers were now not being

answered.

Lonely were the echoes,

And mocking was the laughter.

Terror and bewilderment queued up to come after

Delirium tremens tried to shake me awake!

The beckoning exit was to head for the lake.

I found myself naked at dawn on the shore,

Relief was the feeling to be closing the door.

Sandwiched between life and death,

I entered the water from whence I had come,

Seeking a return to oblivion.

Oblivion was not to be,

A rejected suicide that was me.

In no man's land without a name,

Full of fear and guilt and eternal shame,

I struggled to find the way.

Cross referenced Bible with Book of Mormon,

Aquarian Gospel and the Dead Sea Scrolls,

The Gita, Ramayana and the Koran,

Blake and Wordsworth and John Donne,

With no fulfillment it went on and on.

Looking for spirit not on the top shelf,

Craving a way to come to myself,

And be at ease with within.

Searched every where out there,

And could not decide-

Then St. Kabir, an old master from India,

Said check what's inside yourself

For the answer -

For what's without is within,

Surrender ego, commence and begin.

So letting go of learnt behavior,

Releasing all the fettered fear,

Trusting in the breath that breathes me

From whence it came?!

Now that's my Dear! My Dear! My Dear!

While basking in the Grá of Gratitude -

A beckoning bell from the express,

Hauntingly I start to hear.

But having heard a warning

I still went on once more,

To repeat with dope,

And to elope on what I called a nature trail.

Meandering slow with a bit of blow,

A tab once in a while,

To bring a smile and eradicate what seemed doom

certainty.

Disturbed, disillusioned and caught in a whirl,

In circles I went denying decay.

My children got older than me every day,

Embarrassed for having and addicted Papa,

Underground in a cave like Ali Baba,

With bohemian people frequenting the door,

They were there in the morning asleep on the floor.

Artists, actors, writers, poets and musicians,

Hot airing their theories of how life should just be,

And there in their midst was a self deprived, lonely auld me,

Groping again for reality.

Remembering back to sober and clean,

The answer within was clear to be seen

Surrender and share,

Lay out myself bare.

Why should I care?

I have to be me,

Just be.

Sin é anois - that's it now.

Back Alley Bliss

In a back alley with broken bricks

And cracked pavements

Among left over people who couldn't get in,

I was glad to sit and wait and be at home

Within myself.

Breathing deep and slow a grace seemed to blow

The last of my attachments.

I felt within me grow a love, a warming glow.

Contentment swelled and settled -

And I know for sure that I am happy,

Still happy now as I was then

While waiting for that shining man.

And then he came and he shone and shone

And the sight of him, will always

Linger on and on.

For 'twas he that showed me how to see

What was really me,

That brought me peace and satisfaction

For me, to be, alone, with me,

And love.

October 13th 1984

Like no other

A day like no other was yesterday,

Privileged I was to experience such joy.

While the man that shining man,

No longer is a boy,

But grown, grown into an

Extraordinary man.

How extra beyond measure

Nothing could quantify, diminish,

Or multiply or remotely compare

To that aware one.

Shine he still does

And even more so yesterday

Than some thirty something years ago

When I was struck,

Yes struck dumb and blissed

Content fulfilled and speechless

And even more so yesterday

Still spilling over into today.

I continually swallow the lumps

Of joy and emotion that arise within

To be blessed and alive to know.

To know, that love

Abounds and resides within-

To be seen, heard, felt and tasted

And thereby to be satiated.

Annihilated by bliss,

I just mutter and stutter

In a grinning gratitude

For what he has shown me,

And for that key he gave me

Just to me, for me

To unlock me,

And all for free.

That's* "Fior Grá" like no other.

Maharaji again Barcelona April 3rd. 2011.

*True Love

A Broken Promise

Yes, I know !

I said I would never forsake you!

I did!

I promised to smoke you

 Gon**ja**,.   JA to the end.

You came,

At a time, when I was vulnerable,

I was suffering,

And in need of help.

Pitiful I was,

 In my neediness of anaesthesia.

Obliteration of the senses,

 To quell feelings.

To restrain the brain

From going insane,

From turmoil

Of the equation from the invasion.

Something had lodged and taken hold –

Reason was on the seesaw –

"Why"?

Balance the confusion with

"Why Not".

Angry at a failing hypocritical system,

"Kennedy was dead" !

"Fidel and Che"!?,

 Maybe another way!

The hope, and only friend left, I had to cope.

Daiquiris with Hemingway,

 Had deserted and failed.

Eccentrically addressing myself in barroom mirrors,

Seemed to invite white coated men,

Men from the shadows,

To inveigle,

Disturbing rhythms

 In my eternal internal soliloquies.

With liver sore-hard,

 Cheeks and nose swollen,

Purple veined and blotched,

Bacchus took leave

 And left my Penates,

Vacuuming a space,

A space for cannabinoid replacement.

Solace, for Sole Mio,

You were no doubt,

In those early days,

A drink

For the dry drunk syndrome.

You made gentle, a front row forward,

And brought peace

To a breakfast table.

You put a signpost at the crossroads

To drop out from sick society

And join the peat bog soldiers,

Ploughing on towards self sufficiency

In a grand meitheal

Of artisan comhluadar,

Where free love would upstage

Collapsing, corrupt Catholicism.

You promised Heaven,

You delivered

Seven out of ten.

Then you lured towards the brink

With half-measure focus,

Muddle- think!.

You left me high and dry,

With my face up to the sky

Calling for a rope,

 Or the hope

Of some new dope

Something that delivered

Ease.

Ease to the dis-ease that plagued me.

Attempting to abide

And hide outside

Among my fellow men

To appear and behave like them,

To me

Seemed like an offering of self

To a slave auction,

With a multinational master.

I am not for sale,

So back to my own slave master.

Every mood-altering substance is for me disaster,.

No thanks.

December 2010

The Sun God Ra

The sun god Ra radiates and rectifies

And restores my depleted cells

My spirit rallies to appreciate the replenishment

I nod in affirmation and confirmation

In my reliance on such a god.

A ray from Ra

Would raise that last hurrah!

Before my body into hopeless battle plunge

To pluck hope and freedom light

From dour darkness and blackest night

To expand a hope into a dream

And make what seem impossible achievable

And doable for the merest mortals

The meekest acceptance transmuted to

Mightiest movement of inevitable change

A seed with heat and hydrogen and oxygen

Those primary elements from whence all came

Continues to proclaim the ongoing ness of this
creation.

'Shur isn't it great to be alive and know it.

12/3/09.

Transference!

Moldy empire buildings

Of sooty gray

And red brick dirt,

That housed the gentry,

Of yesteryear,

Your days are numbered

In your rule by fear.

Big Ben's death knell,

Is drawing near.

The city gents

With their bowler hats,

Their rolled umbrellas

And spotless spats,

That made the market

Drop and fall,

And kept the poor

Against the wall.

The tide is turning

On those Eton chaps,

Britannia rules only antique maps

'Tis gas to see, what used to be,

The pride of Her Great Majesty.

The bulldog's balls

Are dragging the ground,

Constantly paranoid,

And circling round,

In an effort to find,

His own lost tail,

Trimmed while plundering

Bunny colonies*.

'Tis a dirty scéal†.

September 1984

* Bunny colonies - a fascist racist term used in
Britain in the 1950s.

Echoes of Piaf in early' 64

A lonely lad tanked up for courage

Went

Searching for love

In the back streets of Nice,

In alleys,

 Where the echoes of Piaf's plaintiff strains,

Clawed the hollows of unrequited passion-

Thirty francs noveau found a girl from the shadows.

My sparrow

Was not six months gone

While I sought her resurrection.

To hold her still,

And calm her fluttering ,

And soothe her aching loneliness.

I got high heels with full frontal

And an admonishment for too much drink

 Caused a long delay from the Irlandais.

(when Rue du France was frequented)

Friendly Old Town

The smell from the Cafe window

Allows me to relax and partake

In the community and commercial interaction

Of my neighbors here in Vieux Nice.

This center hub where I sit has,

Rue St.Francoise,Rue St.Claire,Rue Droite,and Rue

du Collet,

(My present abode) converging with

Restaurants,Cafes,Bars,

Jewelers,Clothes and Cosmetic Shops.

The conversation buzz is suddenly interrupted

By the bub,bub,bub punctuation sounds of an old

Harley Davidson,

Festooned in chrome, painted in bright aqua marine,

matching

The sky line of wooden shutters up to six stories high

with

The occasional clothes line displaying the french

exotic

And colorful panache of practical undergarments .

My young waitress,blonde and beautiful,

Her large gold earrings, equal in

Diameter to the bubble she blows

With an innocent impudence, to display

Her brash exuberance and youthful liberty,

And then sucked in for further mastication

And possibly some considered contemplation,

Of what possibilities this day holds in store.

Tall slim monsieur attired ,

In white and cream with straw fedora

Pauses to observe his surroundings

While a fresh baguette pokes clear from

His plastic bag of lettuce and green peppers,

The darkening sky he observes before

Striding upwards along Rue St.Claire.

The sensual lady in red secure in her voluptuousness

Has again retreated down Rue du Collet with her

Rotund and darkly attired proud companion,

She shimmies and flexes her buttocks

As she brushes her designer bottom

With ring-less long slender fingers,

She tilts her head with a smirk of certainty

And recent fulfillment in her femininity.

A scarlet slash framing white even teeth in

Semi pouting lips bids all admirers silently adieu.

Some spatters of light rain have now

Thinned the pavement perambulators

And left mainly lunch time diners,

Beer sippers and cafe loungers like myself

Lingering with shoulders scrunched under the canopies

And umbrellas as the wind clacks and flaps loudly

The most dilapidated aqua marine wooden shutters

From on high.

5/10/2010.

Heralding Freedom

The sun shines bright behind my head,

White grey hairs reflect the light

And shield my working cells

Within the cranium, my prison, where lurks

My jailer or my chaperone,

Depending on the moon! the moon!

The weather - Aie!

That's how it is.

Spring's on the way and

Patrick's Day not far away

And still no chits planted.

A different year 'twill be

For me, to see this brand new me

That I never met before,

An adult free and joyful in sobriety.

That darlin' woman who graced my bed

With her affectionate care and sensuality

Has been breakfasted, now gone to work

And left lingering a tingling of her laughter.

To be alive and hopeful for new season's promise,

Is to me a step upon the springboard of eternity

A dawn emerging from the Kaliyuga.

Heralding freedom from frenzied fury.

A skip step from a child,

About to jump in time -

It's the hand of God that twirls the rope

And bids adieu to the reign of Pope

And all the christian crusaders

That murdered with impunity.

Historians that hid behind the impremator

On their degreed' diplomas,

Will be exposed full frontally for

Complicity in concealing truth.

Clerics that crowned the kings,

And kings that crowned the clerics,

So the masses could be manipulated,

Controlled and regulated,

Taxed, axed, and terminated.

The blood that flowed down the front

Of the chalice,

Could be seen on the surplice soutanned,

Vested in malice.

Behind the confessional door of the secrets,

The power mad celibates stunned and steered

The minds of the people

With an imperial adage of

Divide and conquer.

They milked dry the joy of

God's love.

Ah! but now the spring has returned,

Some seven thousand seasons later,

An ember fanned so cautiously

Despite the scourges through the ages

Flickers to flame.

A sacred heart that's full of joy,

And not crowned with thorns and sorrow,

But a man that turned the tables on the bankers,

And called most high priests a shower of wankers.

"An Earraig anseo anois" with caution towards

tomorrow.

Tuesday March 12th 2002

Divorce!? Distractions

Looking through the window at Poll na Róm,

Snow on the ground, soundless crunch,

Hollow echo surrounds the thermal man.

Black is white to day -

Outside at least.

Inside anguish warms the suffering heart,

For fear it might enjoy a brief respite.

Time ticks in the hall,

Super-Ser lights one of the three yokes

And crinkles with its clinker sound,

A thermostat clicks to herald the roar

Of a burner rushing in,

It gets it's rhythm by the count of four

And holds a muffled din.

The mind flicks in,

The eyes search round for some distraction

To lead away from pain within,

It fixes on a patch of sky

A bird flies by - imagination follows him -

To fly through snow - why must he go?!

Some social errand maybe? or kin?

St. Francis caught the vibe I know,

He watched the birds neither reap nor sow.

I wonder do they sing some hymn?

Some distant melody from ages past,

To regenerate primordial sound,

And spark awareness to those on ground,

A consciousness I scarce can speak,

My mind is too fixed on reap on reap.

To reap a harvest I have not sown,

To take, to keep, to call my own,

I wish to God I had only known!

Before they had flown!

Me thinks, perhaps that man will kill

All little birds that fly and sing,

With all their waste that's in the skies,

Pollution, acid rain, insecticides.

That chain may well be broken

From ground to air and all that reigns

May be despair,

Unless man opens up his heart to share

What's real, what was always there,

The space to love, to trust, to care.

17th December 1982

Belated Identification

A young man with a bullhorn loudspeaker is
vociferously declaring
His objections to and regarding
Recently planned and current government pension
policies.
He respectfully addresses an assembled crowd in
Place Massena in centre city Nice.
The mixed aged and mixed colour gathering
Applaud his sentiments, his utterances, and his
rhetoric,
All while red banners are unfurled and songs and
slogans
Of freedom are audibly brandished
And delivered in deliberate dignity,
In determined certitude of forthcoming action.
While meanwhile, nearby-
The strollers stroll, the cyclists cycle,
While a little boy has his young athletic father,
Right in the palm of his hand.
A magic moment is there to view-

Watching the two communicate-

The little fellow knows for sure he is loved,

Loved without stint, and therefore is complete.

The young father is totally bedazzled and befuddled

By this being he has brought about

And has leashed himself to in passive submission

For the next two decades at the very least.

His own dreams and ambitions step down a notch

And somehow are subconsciously placed

On the little fellows shoulders – to be enjoyed

At some future date with accolades from an adoring

father.

Confusion will reign when the little lad

Will shift his loyalty, to love and possess his mother,

He will ape and cape the old bull

And cause restless nights of anguish, worry and

disillusion.

Eventually he will fall in and out of love

And come forth for comfort, for compassion

From the father he helped to educate in feeling

feelings.

The young father pauses now and then while they
play
They both listen and tune to the bullhorn rhetoric,
And then he hoists the son on his shoulders
While they both cheer! "Vive la Liberte".

12th.October 2010 at 14.15. (I salute you young
people of France)

<u>Kingdom's Princess</u>

The Kingdom's princess Maria,

Today co-joined with

The Tribe's King Bill.

Setting off on their life's journey,

Most of us crossed seas to wish them well.

Beneath the clear blue skies of Altea,

Underneath the scorching sun,

In the little chapel on the hill,

A gorgeous young woman

Strolled up the aisle on her father's arm,

Her protector from harm he has been

Until now.

And now his Adam's apple

Palpitated perceptibly with his

Frequent swallowing as he

Prepared to surrender his

Youngest daughter.

Chriostoir O'Murchu had

A tear in his eye

Which he himself would deal with

Bye and bye.

The bridegroom at the alter

Was anxious but steady,

His turn to take over and cherish

Was ready.

Giolla an Bringloid.

Little tinkling bells that sound so sweet and
comforting
Still ring within, rejuvenating the memory of her
gentle laughter .
Her strong but soft and toil worn hands
I feel their touch and cherish a moment of their pause
and patience.
Why am I intrigued, beguiled, swallowing emotions
In the hope that they may not be dissipated.
This French woman cajoled the cajoler
While smiling among the swaying palm trees of
Kerala.
Oh! Lord but she took captive a near stifled heart
Held it lovingly beside her own pain
And kindly kindled a spark of hope.
This spark is still so gently fanned to glimmer and
glide
Crossing an ocean in a "bringloid "a dream and
carries back
An angel!

Please let me help this angel find its wings!

Am I dwindling away a sixty year old in decay?

Will I die in my footsteps before the heart rot festers

And hangs me up like an effigy

A scare crow figure gone ragged with emotional

throwaways

That flow like weed seed on the wind

Over a barren wasteland ,hostile in their indifference

To life or death.

Austin your face in death still haunts me

To stroll alone without the drumbeat of the fellowship

Is a lonely path.

To imagine myself as an ordinary Joe

As being free of this killer disease

Is to undermine reality .

Reality, precious, but painful is passing slowly

Presently.

(La Rochelle 18th. December 2001.)

<u>Feelings</u>

Sometimes I feel so tall
When my ego is small
And my heart is full
Of joy and gratitude
For being gifted with the
Little me in me.
To see from a place
Of wide vision
Where there is more in the frame
Than just me,
And my wants,
And my cares,
And my worries.
Where all is just perfect
Exactly where its meant to be
Right now.

13/7/09.

I flew

I flew before I grounded,

Crashed and crushed,

I lost my nerve

To try or fly again.

The nerve ends frizzled and frazzled

Over generations of existence thru millennia

Leaving only memory

Lingering longings in imagination..

I scud the ceilings

Above the clouds

Lurking ,prying ,peering

Among the bodyless beings

Who clamour in cacophony

Yowling for yet another chance

At life in human form.

Light Lingam Warning

A foreskinless candy striped barber pole lighthouse

Protrudes rude and nude over Kovlam beach

It sits astride that rock

That rock that runs out west to sea

And was the source of protection

A Krisnoffer safety belt on the Stephen's Day

Tsunami.

Shiva brought the wave to the door

But no more.

It lapped a warning ,

That had been grapevined to nearby Varkala

By a jungle drum that cleared

The people from the beach

Just as Hanumans viewpoint between Kanu Kumari

and Lanka

Filtered the alarm warnings

As also Ganesh did to his elephant kin ,

To break their chains of bondage

And head for higher ground .

Meanwhile western technology gas grumbled

And war mumbled.

Is that the Bell?

The last lap, what will it be ?

Puff and pant and maybe I'll see?

A glimmer of light smiling hope to me?

Struggling for breath?

Or maybe?

A second wind to take another inhalation

As if it were my last,

To cherish the moment where eternity began

Never ceasing to unfold its miracles,

From seed to stem, to leaf, to flower, to fruit,

To rot to nourish the seed to root, to stem and

Maybe see the fruit of labour and love

Come to flower in this Garden of Eden.

A trembling gratitude I feel to be the me

That sees from behind my eye out,

Way out there, where beings long for love,

And the truth within,

Yet spend their life in search without-

All in a moment a flash

An igneous spark, an instant

Where there is no time for reflection or shadow,

A brief glimpse of raw reality

There is now and nothing more

Being there with full heart and soul,

Body and mind,

Grateful for perception

To know I am living,

And this body is going to die.

"a comforting certainty"

Who Was She At All

Who was she at all?

Oh! Yes, she was my first God!.

Intense security on the out breath,

Followed shortly by intense insecurity on the

inbreath.

Such was existence for me as a child with Mamma..

My father's advice to me was

To keep my mind to myself like a pig rooting.

However, good advice went unheeded by the child,

Who wished to eat tomorrow,

Before digestion of yesterday.

Insatiable I was for information

On who, why, what, when, and whether

All this made sense and came together.

She tried when she had time, to

Bring logic, truth and rationale

To foggy, misty, and diffuse realms of

Supposed mystical and religious education.

Her views were her own,

Differing from the drivel dogma force fed

To minors –and so a question mark

Was not so dark, but a quirk to be encouraged

And for that I thank you Maie my mother.

But who was she this mother of mine?

She that could not keep still

And constantly battled to improve beauty

For the beholder..

A critical eye remained held at bay,

In abeyance, for the day when she would utter

Her very own unique view.

Men loved the feisty, sparky, sparkly,

Fashionably intense whirlwind energy, and

intelligence

That always spun in her vicinity.

All lines were clear cut,

Precise bold definitely defined,

Without ambiguity!

And if you couldn't see it –you were dense.

Her misty eye that gazed towards the middle distance

Would snap back to the present tense with such

impatience,

T hat she could make one feel guilty for time wasting

As one awaited her direction on what one's next

chores were.

God she was A Deva no doubt!

Yes, Yes, she would shout and tell you

In no uncertain terms

What you were about ,

And what you weren't about,

All with a withering look ,.

Reducing you to a very ignoble status.

She would rant on about a heritage emanating

Ignorance, obtuse and lacking

Background and breeding traits,

Prominent in your father's family.

So leaving you without a leg to stand on

You carefully maintained a dwarf stature

In her vicinity, when she was in one of her moods!

Now moods were like clouds across an Irish sky,

They were unpredictable, numerous,

Dark, fleeting, feathery fine,

Or Offenbachish howling from the underworld

Of Celtic submission and suppression,

Full of resentment from the Roman shadow.

The Saracen head on her family Coat of Arms

Held some mysterious significance for her

Whereby she parasolled proudly in her superiority

And her disdain of the "noveau riche"

While at all times she maintained an agreeable
familiarity

With good blood stock breeders,

And hard working tillage farmers.

Her father's "sheaf of wheat "trade mark

Was some badge of great distinction,.

She was a child once

Was my mother, or so she said

With my uncle Tom, her little older brother

They had such fun when they were young

When, there only was the two of them,

On the arrival of the goddess Diana

Then Seán, Neans, Brenedan and Joseph.

Childhood had ended and

Work was to be done by someone

And who was the one!.

The convent offered sanctuary for this bright spark

Or this smouldering inferno, where within she did
consider
Serving that dynamic force of energy-
That intense vitality that so propelled her.
While prayer pondering, on vows and vocation,
She encountered equal intelligence, and innocence
Perusing the poetry shelves in the Thurles library.
It was there cute cupid caused confusion and
My father Jack got smitten and
Became her ever loving slave protector.
 Their minds seemed to wrestle incessantly thereafter
While concurrence agreed occasionally, and harmony
Hovered spasmodically during project manoeuvres
Made sure she did that everyone knew that
She had built our house in Thurles
Detached it was, with a round window
And curved porch roof , high walls and gates
Proclaiming privacy from neighbours,
But plain people came to live near by,
And so we moved again to the capital
Where big intentions were intent and
Swiftly put in motion.

A corner detached house it had to be

In Dublin 3, convenient to bus,

Train, beach and sea, golf club and rugby,

Then she at last could so attend the College of Art

Where there she'd spend her leisure in pleasure.

Then ghosts came home, with a print of Guernica

Inside the door, a revolution in the hall,

With Picasso on the wall,

While elementals paced the floor,

They would utter lines and be heard no more ,

The Gate the Abbey with Michael Mac Liammor

And Hilton E, with light entertainment from Jimmy O

Dea,

Then the Cruiscean Lán from Myles na G,

Sardonic lines from Kavanagh P while the Bishops

Bonfire

Blazed high from O'Casey , and the Quare Fella

Questioned capital punishment and justice, from

Brendan B.

Consequently mealtime discussions ,to say the least

Had rations of passion ,and lashings of controversy.

Yes yes my mother got her say..

Miniatures were deftly painted, clay pots and shapes
Moulded were thrown fired and glazed
Colours gleamed and were fashionably in vogue
To be superseded by something more exotic.
Change was the constant with fashion and style
Proclaimed from high heeled spikes and millenary
magnificence,
A real dazzler for Sunday communion
Where she stood six foot tall in a shapely five foot
mass.
Then a business woman came to the fore,
Antiques she'd sell through her front door,
So you learned to detach from your favourite
armchair
As you would likely return and find it not there..
Silver, porcelain, crockery and delph
Chippendale, Sheraton. Gilt golden mirrors and
clocks,
Ming dynasty from China, fine art from France,
Nothing was stable you held on to your pants.
Excitement ran rife while deals were being made,
What held precedence was Christies, Sotheby's,

Adams Auctions, Louis Wines,the Trade.

Her cohort John Jacob the Jew man

Called in twice a year

His Comer van in the driveway

For items to clear.

Turnover she would have with profit big or small

Business was business on the ball in the hall,

When the bell rang you silenced ,

Got swiftly out of the way

The queen bee took over

And Maie had her say! That was the way.

Her boys were reared,

And the youngest had his practice,

So down to Galway she had to come,

To supervise, and oversee her grandchildren.

While overlooking the ocean one morning from his
bedroom,

Jack took his leave of her-

Just after breakfast while she lit the two

One for herself and the other for the smiler,

The other, that never got puffed!.

She was brave and diligent, determined and decisive,

Having picked her plot in Rahoon Cemetery,

Surveying Clare and Galway Bay..

Inward she went for those last two years,

Moved house again, and went back to her maiden
name,

Despising the inept taxman

Who funded and fondled the corrupt politicians

Enabling the shylock bankers and slithery barristers.

Back then she spoke of Saint Mary Magdalene ,

And the Little Flower- Saint Theresa,

While her last words to me was a quote from
"Thoreau"

"Beware of the men in suits".

Her end was tragic,

Having had a stroke,

She had to smoke,

Addiction was her downfall

For a matchstick broke alight

And torched her funeral pyre

Which she tried to quench

But her heart gave out

And thereby she did expire.

She nestled in beside Jack in Rahoon Cemetry,

On a cold and bleak spring noon

To the strains from the Uilleann pipes

Of Eugene Lamb, playing her favourite "Sliabh na

mBan".

On her tombstone we put some of her favourite lines

Of Edna St.Vincent Millay,

"My candle burns at both ends

It will not last the night,

But ah! My foes !

And oh! My friends

It gives a lovely light."

I love and miss you Maie my mother,

And when I think of you some lines from

 Another of your favourites "Amy Lowell"

From "Shooting the Sun"

Later in the week 'tis due
North that I would hurry to.

While on other days I find
To the South content of mind.

So I start but never rest
North or South or East or West.

Each horizon has its claim
Solace to a different aim.

Four –souled like the wind am I,
Voyaging on an endless sky,
Undergoing destiny."

Who was she at all?
Oh! yes she was my first God.

Little Boy

The little boy I love so much

And for so long as I remember

His open face with question eyes

So pure in their young innocence

Looms before the door of my

Heart's longing.

To feel his little fingers clutch,

To smell his unique scent,

And be warmed by his puff pant

Breath upon my neck

Is to me a taste of paradise.

Oh! Muirgheas little friend of mine

That I had longed for all these years

I love you more than ever.

Thru his little window

What wondrous sights are seen ?

He seems to be content and happy,

With what seems to be and what has been.

Lying supine in sedate and splendorous slumber

His even breath shushing through

His tiny little nostrils

With kitchen sounds making background

To his dreams .

Tis with freshness he encounters and not

With habit every day

Each moment is an new beginning

With full potential on the way.

30/12/'84

__Grandma__

O grandma whom I never knew,

I feel you were quite kind,.

I have heard you spoke most softly,

And were of gentle mind .

No prideful airs and graces,

You just liked to darn socks,

As the grandad went to bed early,

Having wound up all the clocks.

Having read his sermon from the mount,

And seemed sometimes, to rule by fear,

You showed your patience and your love,

By always being near,

Close by, to calm the waters,

And cool the troubled air.

You got your peace at nighttime,

While your man was up the stair.

Spent your life in family service

And so rarely got acclaim

In shadowed glory bore a family,

There was none who took your name.

It must have been a mans world,

I n those days long ago,

And here I am your grandson,

Who'd just really like to know

What you dreamed? and what you thought of

Where you fancied just to be ?

In a town or in a city?,

In a country where 'twas free,

Free to be yourself love,

In a simple peasant way,

Trusting Nature that surely loved you,

Tynagh's child,right through-

Adieu Roscrea.

Autumn '83.

Alhambra 6<u>th</u>. May 09

Delightful gardens with sea stone patterned cobbled
walkways
Conical cypresses proliferate and inspire
The Muslim man to spread his seed and
Look down on the grandiose Granada.
*'God is great and made the world
But the builder built the houses.'
A lot of work well designed to distribute
Life giving water to trees, shrubs and plants
That gave shade shelter and sweet scent
To the inhabitants.
Impressive structures
Manifesting magnanimity in monument
And moment not to be discarded
Lightly by minions on lower slopes.
Echoes of the Taj Mahal and the Red Fort
Are indeed perceptible as one meanders
Through the chambers and loving quarters
And then the Roman room suffused in gloom
Shrouded square in shaped design

Hungry and hollow

Inquisition to follow.

a quote from a four year old Denise O'Connell in 1970.

<u>Wo Who</u>

Oh! Breath and energy that waited and took flesh

And went on to be what I call me, thanks!.

That little part that I rarely show

And barley know

But that I feel is truly me

Come forward and find a voice

And say what it is to be

Incarcerated in this human form

Unacknowledged by the world domain

Yet clinging on by a tendril of love

In a flimsy fragile firmament.

A tiny spark of light in the blackest night

Shines forth a hope for fulfilment's longing,

A gonging resonating in the very fibres

Of my being and heart's desire

To be

To be

To be at rest by my own home fire,

Warming self in the basking sunshine

Of a mind at peace

The hay saved and the harvest in store,

The children fed and the wife in bed

Awaiting the resurrection.

The re-creation and recreation from fornication

And the joy of just being Abel and not Cain.

Without teeth in Torrevieja

Noontime Tues 21st.April '09

Here I am sitting out in the sunshine
Overlooking the sea
On the promenade in Torrevieja .
I am at the extreme end finally
Away from the vendors
Amidst local dog strollers
Residents no doubt of this
Magnolia high rise apartment block
Behind me .
Some tradesman is tapping away
Seemingly content at his work
Presumably tiling
And feeling lonely as he echoes
His voice "in sole mio style"
To an imaginary audience
And then to pause
While he sorts out another

Bundle of clackers.

A fishing boat opposite

Is dispensing net from its stern

As it chugs towards the west

With the wind behind it.

The lapping sound of water splashing

On the rocky foreshore is soothing.

The scrunching sound on the gravel walkway

Proclaims another canine

Exercising his homo sapiens.

A little later having need of something soothing

For my vacant gums

I venture back towards vendors.

Puerta de la Libertad

At the end of the long board walk

The hum and chatter from

Side walk cafes cover the sound

Of sea slapping on green brown rocks

Ice cream cone lickers face

Out to sea comfortable on the free benches.

Skaters swish by psychedelically attired

In designer sports gear.

Cheeky bummed waitresses

Usher strollers assertively towards

Their tables and wares

While a local weather-beaten

Fisherman pedals his bike

With his protruding three rods

Home for what's on offer at Siesta time-knowing a sprat

Would catch a salmon.

Son Sanchez,sa naturlemente

Beams in colourful graffiti

From a facing wall-reminding one

Of Mexican conquests long ago.

A bronze statue of a sailor in southwester

With gyroscoped compass, rope and anchor

Stands astride a stone cobblers last

Scanning the eastern horizon.

A child from his pushchair harangues

And hollers in more scream

For ice-cream..

The Obsessionist

The reflex claw springs from a possessive hunger to devour
To consume and subsume the inner spirit
And make it your own.
A vacuum hollow in the brain it calls home
Lurks in the shadows constantly silently prowling
Insatiable for comfort feasting of forbidden pleasures.
Yes reluctantly I admit to the continued existence
And the constant subliminal nurturing of the shadow self ,
But self, with its multitude of complicit dimensions, remain
Narciousictly boxed in a chamber of mirrors and lenses.
The reptilian energy that took flight from the Garden
Nestling there in flying dragon form among the seven sisters,
Six of whom shine bright especially at equinoxes

Those beautiful alluring whispering maidens ever
beguiling,

While the misty one ,one so rarely seen holds sway in
secret .

The question mark pendulum swinging between
fantasy or perceived reality

Staggers betimes and sometimes spirals its
holographic images into

The old memory banks still festering with guilt and
remorse

Products of the substitute ,"that vino veritas" that
"Spiritus Santus"

Whose whereabouts we were told came from without

Whereas in fact it was always there fluttering within

Recognisable only by the loving pure heart...

What's this Venus in the middle of the Pleiades !!
2012

Angel's Highway

I sat at the edge of the ocean while the lightly lapping waves shushed the sand and pebbles with a soothing rhythm, attempting to pull my limbs into a half lotus like posture proved pitiful as the knees and ankles were no longer as supple as my mind was about the passing of time. Closing my eyes, inhaling long and deep through both nostrils, holding, retaining still holding I attempt to hear with my temples, pausing before exhaling fully with vigour and closing and pausing again before inhaling and listening to the singing sound within. Breathing in and out in rythmetic contentment, my eyes closed my thoughts marshal themselves and want to ramble and go spacing but years of practice at herding them back to the corral the energy is focused on breath energy before my backbone and somehow I am in suspension.

A gentle warmth envelops me and I release all the tension that I use to bind my mind and its attachments. I open my eyes the sun is close to setting over the ocean and we are linked by the dazzling pathway the shimmering palanquin of reflected refractions of the sacred sunlight - the angels' highway - is evident before me. Mesmerized I gaze like a child and I revel in my own bedazzlement and I indulge in my indulgence.

I close my eyes and the after image lives on and on and on as I breathe with it, and travel and travel, deep, deep, deep within
In ainm Dé
In ainm Dé
In ainm Dé
Solus Dé
Dé Light
Ah yes! ag dul abhaile!

Along the angels highway when my departure comes
about,
I hope to take my leave from here
And go without a shout or doubt.
That my life's yearnings,
My great wish to just come home
And be with Mother Nature,
Alive and all alone.
All alone without attachments
Free to soar like the falcon high
Like a grain of sand across the desert
Like the blue that's in the sky
Oh! How this spirit loves to fly.
Fly away from all the maya,
This illusion called the world
By myriads in the media
"Slaveens" of the absurd
"Ignorami" of the "word."

In the beginning there was energy
Known by Gnostics as a sound,
The *Om*, the first vibration

Before matter came to town.

Back then when I was simpler

And there wasn't much around

Just air and ether

'Twas the friction made the sound,

The sound - that sound that's still around.

Along the Angel's Highway

I hope to dance my soul's departure

Merging in the bright sun rays,

Infinitesimal in the dark,

Lonely echoes in the night dogs bark.

Yes it will be my spirit twilight cruising,

Reaching out to souls in pain,

Let them not depart in vain,

But realise what is *religio*,

That their temple is within,

And trusting in the breath that's there now,

Surrender fully and begin.

Begin.   *November 2nd 2004*

Beached

I watched a little girl cling to her daddy,

As he walked without worry,

Content in his parenting,

And I was transported back,

Back, three and twenty years ago,

They are now out of sight and have gone on.

I am left listening to the waves beating the shore,

Wondering what happened to my little stór,

my valentines gift child from Cappamore.

The day she was born I was present, all there,

I rythmed her tiny feet to let her know there was care,

The same as I had done when she was within,

While I had sung and played with her mother

Who was no longer thin.

Stood watch on the dark nights

When it was stormy without,

Got bested with tirade and continuous shout

From a mother uncertain of just how to be

With and infant needing stroking,

Touching, cuddling, - a needy baby.

Those big eyes that probed the depths of my soul,

As I held her and rocked her to feel rhythm and roll.

We clung to each other in uncertainty,

Knowing that love kept us wanting to be, and be.

Now being, I am, and where be, is she?

Gone stateside I'm told,

There is no contact with me.

Sometimes I get lonely, and wonder why so?

You love someone so dearly and off they just go.

12/6/2009.

Maybe

Maybe you can't remember,

Or maybe you were unaware,

Or it just maybe that you don't care,

But I remember.

Those wind howling nights,

When your mother was tired

And you were awake seeking attention-

A wet nappy, a cuddle,

A bit of wind, an unsettling dream

Loving arms were there to hold you

To carry you out to see the moon,

To see the stars and view the Milky Way,

While always listening quietly

To the night dogs bark, or

A fox from far away.

Putting fresh sticks on the fire

In the wee small hours of the morning.

That was our time for little stories,

And old songs with half remembered lines

And gentle rhymes to pass the time,

Until you were ready to sleep again

And you'd stretch and yawn

And close your eyes,

And you'd pat me

With your tiny little hand,

Letting me know it was time..

Time, to put you back to bed.

It is sad now, if all is said.

(Remembered again in June 2010)

<u>Uniqued</u>

Uniqued by conception

I am birthed to enjoy,

Day by day,

Year by year,

One moment at a time

My life-

That experience

That is happening right now

Within me.

I am privileged to be

One at one

Connected to the source

That distributes the gifted

Feelings of aliveness

Calm and still

Yet unequivocally linked

To the perpetuale mobilae of novelty,

Freshness and freedom in opportunity –

And all this long before I read or write

Or believe in anybody-

And now!!

Do I go backwards from here?

Shackled to the world

And what it seemingly offers?

Or breathe on and know now,

What I experienced then.

27th.September 2006.

"seo é anois"

Springtime Spacing on Sliabh Carron

To conjure past,

Make fast,

And hold the vein (of consciousness.)

A butterfly of red,

With circles blue on wings outspread,

A mate to join the fun

Proclaimed the day.

Two pheasants on the roadway,

A field lit with primrose yellow

Wafting breeze with scented air,

A warm firm hand and steady gait

To cross the jigsawed rock

And climb to patch of gentian blue

And azure hue

Lay down to gaze,

Amaze.

Suspended breath,

Time waits as eyes meet,

To share a treasure rare,

Naught need be said

As hearts disrobe to dance entwined,

Still shy of simple harmony.

Sun's rays diffused by scudding clouds

Prompts move to upward climb

Cross Hazel Crag

Still bare in birthing bud

In expectation of green canopy.

Where blue bells grow in shaded light,

Manured by wild goats' pebbles,

Where a herd had rested in its shelter,

Perhaps to mate and comfort

Thru a winter storm

In wild garlic scented crevices.

While an upward lure to pant once more,

Seek out and find the pinnacle,

Soft shade of pink from orchid pure,

Resplendent in its vigor,

Captivated and enthralled two souls,

Who clasped to entwine fingers

In unison, to stoop together,

Enraptured by such simple beauty.

Light warm pink lilac hint of aura

From so many sheltered, nooky little crevices -

Stopped time again

To bring primordial memory back to the dawn of first

creation.

Like two children who are on mitch from school,

Who share something rare and special.

1984 (I wish I remembered her name, a lovely

premie* back from Japan.)

Scanning Still Steele in Scandinavia

Silent sterile with snow sound!

A country on hold,

Awaiting?!

Significantly proclaiming literacy

Coaxing consumers' co-operation

Subtly implying by implanting a dutiful debt

Subliminally for monarchic benevolence

In a neutral, social opulence.

Gliding swiftly from Stockholm

Outward through Solentuna,

Towards the steel town.

I observe lots of trees and

Abandoned machinery.

Outside in the snow, a tinkers' paradise,

A sheer fortune to be made in scrap metal,

Shadows of a by-gone age of industrial opulence

Now seemingly in decline.

A strange type of substrata society

Prevails and lurks in reservation.

The eyes follow in observation,

Without the betrayal of any feelings or emotions.

A detached coolness seems to be prevalent fashion.

The majority of adults seem constricted and
constipated,

While the odd alpha female

Will look you in the eye

And smile invitingly without restriction.

A demonstration of strength

Security and a social confidence

Balancing beauty with benign benevolence,

Telling me that eventually some slaves

Overcome their captors.

Time ticks more slowly here in the Northland,

Where adults speech is more measured,

Children chatter readily, probably

Exercising frozen facial muscles for warmth,

While calling for approval.

Dog numbers have definitely declined

Up here in distant Dalarana

While this lone wolf retraces

Tracks well frozen now by two score years and more,

Still prowling,

Still howling!

Hearing only echoes!

Broken Link.

Memory of a trust betrayed

Has power to break the will to live

And leave one subdued in nothingness,

Where and when only then

Can a new fresh start

To placate the heart,

Be entered new.

Trust who?

Older,

Faded memory-youth,

Scythe man shadows

And awaits his certain harvest.

Let's hope,

It be not bitter fruit,

Let one pure drop of love remain,

To bloom a rose,

To say,

I knew.   Spring '83.

Bate that Trinity College.

Eduard Cournane from Butler Avenue,

A light gentle genius

Of kind tongue and astute mind,

You ministered diligently to all and sundry

Regardless of the pay,

And come what may in fair

And foul weather you came to the needy.

Your Reilly motar car was to be seen

Careering down many a bumpy bohereen

To far afield farm houses.

Your internal dialogue

Must have been in tune,

For you smiled a lot

Despite the gloom of dark dictate

In a cathedral town.

I remember you to hum along

While reciting lines from Dylan Thom

For as a little boy my favorite job

Was traveling on the run board of your car

With alacrity I opened and closed gates,

As we seemed to criss cross half the country.

Quite often in the moonlight

You turned off your main headlights,

Sharpening your night vision,

Maintaining a precision of perception

So you said.

I feel now you were an artist

And just wanted to see more,

Having looked inside the door

Of a play pen den in Ship Street in Shanghai

Inhaling deep the poppy smoke

That I am sure awoke the yen to poke

The fire another fraction higher.

I thank you kind Doctor for your

Time and consideration and all those

Questions answered with patient,

Thoughtful, truthful, respectful, and intuitive

deliberation.

You alone with Mamma's mum made me feel worthy

and welcome,

As I was an insatiably curious ten year old, branded

betimes as very bold.   July '09.

__Paddy Joe__

There's a man I know called Paddy Joe

Who came back from over beyond.

 He has a smile a winsome smile

That can open you like a key,

There is a twinkle in his eye. .

That's there for all to see,

Its sure that man had fun.

Clean cut features from cement dust sweat,

A handclasp you'd be glad to own,

An eye to beauty and to vigor,

That sorta spirit who'd go it alone.

I watch the man stand back..

And once again take stock,

He's disappointed by the way things fared at home,

Since first he'd left to roam.

The crack - what crack !!!!!!

Let me tell you something !!!! ?

Enthusiasm, spirit, vehement determination to have a
go

That spontaneous energy to elevate,

Radiated from the man like an addictive hue

And captivated the attentive respondent.

The whole tremor, buzz and air of a country fair

Would tremble off his lips

With the alacrity of a greyhound after a hare.

He would make time stand still

And he'd smile

A tiny hidden fleck of pain,

And you'd know a lot of that road was uphill.

And he'd smile and you'd know, he'd do it all again.

<u>When Dragons Fly</u>

Two red dragonflies that bounced on the air

Rhythmically they flirted and flitted

Skirting the white spray of the waterfall

They almost touched ten times in

Sixty seconds, they teased and titillated,

They were mad to mate.

I felt their desire- it touched me deep

I gasped with pain and joy-was lonely as

I thought of you,

Wanted you

And thought of you again

And wanted you more.

So I plunged into the cool pool

To drown the desire by swimming down and deep

So I would ache for breath

More than I would long for you.

Yes! it worked for a while but I had to

Surface and breathe again.

Now you have become like air to me

And I want you more than ever.

Neyer Dam, Kerala, January 1997

Its You I See

Its you I see when I look around

Its you I hear through the crashing sea

Its you I scent amidst the jasmine and the sandalwood

I hurt inside with longing-such sweet hurt

Another's eyes laughed into mine –

I laughed back

But it was into yours I gazed,

And a longing squeezed my heart-I was sad.

Oh! How I have searched for you back then

When you did not know me.

Tortured I tossed, tormented for the touch of you

To hear you breathe beside me

I would just listen all night

And wait and wait and wait till the cock crew

And then to doze till sunrise.

Kerala. 26/2/97.

The Genie's Price Tag

The wild-man wants an airing

He has been self bottled far too long

Clinches teeth, not his own, while driving

As some unbridled memories come in strong.

The car is doing sixty down a narrow country road

Where in the past he suffered anguish pain and
overload

The fuck it switch is leering ominously

As the pedal hits the floor

The rev-counter is in the red zone

On the change from three to four,

We are bouncing ninety and some more

This ship is far from shore

With self destruct along the door.

Enter at your own risk!

An angry man is at the helm

With a growling gale inside his head

He does not wish to hurt a body

Yet there is a tempting beckoning from the dead

To surf the line of sheer excitement

Whispering thrill and test the call
Of dead dogs howling in the distance
Like Jerusalem's Wailing Wall.
Grinning gargoyles leer from hedgerows
Careering wildly near the brink
And all this happening with no drink.
No drink, no drink -
Pause a moment and reflect some
Am I living in some past pain?
Slow down and get my bearings
Or 'tis down that road I go again.

<u>Weedy Garden</u>

O weedy garden

Near gone to seed

Your decadent splendour

Reflects my soul.

Variety of wild growth

With tiny flowers of subtle hues

Provide a playground for ladybirds

And hard backed beetles

Who never seemed as content before

When left to march in ordered rows.

Today they move relaxed

No paranoid pressure from hacking hoe

To harm them or their young

The birds of air

Their only foe.

Shure its not so bad

No fear of spray,

Yanky Vietnam nightmare

Has gone away.

16/6/'83

Musky Memories

Musky memories from the monkey mind

Of Mister Adult

Standing in his cot,

Looking aghast at the future

In his past,

Somewhat mesmerised by

The time warp,

And hallucinating views

Elongated in the kaleidoscopic,

Privileged vision of a well fed infant

Silently and sceptically surmising.

The muddied ever shifting version of truth

Being far more real than the delivered version

Being promulgated by the authority in the nursery.

We tip toe through fairy land

Blind man bluffed with fairy tales,

Ever searching for Red Riding Hood,

Questioning all Snow White virginity,

Wishing to be the big bad wolf for once.

The woman with the Lemon Top

The woman with the lemon top

And busting boobs

Her designer white shorts and

Doctor Livingstone white hat

Marches up the beach

Into the middle distance staring.

Disdainfully she looks my way

And kicks some sand

As she passes.

Her gait is that of a dame

Who gets her way

And would make you pay

For every ounce of compassion

I am glad she has passed

And has not dallied

My scrotum scrunched and my

Balls I carried close in for safety.

Her big white arse has cleared

The far dune

And this sandy cove is back

In tune

As the waves that wash and

Lap the shore

And clear the air and

Bring once more

The tune back into harmony.

Updesh

A soaring bird always carries

A little bit of me aloft

That weightless part defying gravity

Yes within I live a life that's separate

In a freedom span that's not confined

To rules, red tape or regulations.

I see the wind and hear the sound from stone

I feel the kiss of the ocean from the rain

I sense the moving heat from the melting snow

And I shimmer in light to vacuum space

Where love alone dances with divinity.

A yes!

A yes!

That other side of me,

That mamma saw thru misty eye

When I was fed, changed and in my bed

Contentedly gurgling I raised my head

An infant paradised in security

In full surrender like a lotus flower

Afloat upon a sea of lovingness

A miracle in evidence.

Beyond the compass bearings

Of north, south, east or west

In longitude, latitude or *updesh

Hitherto uncharted

Is the region where my soul swells

In humble awe and gratitude.

A smile, a smirk uncreases brow

And deletes the power of government.

I skip with joy to be the boy

I longed to be in childhood

Where a breath of air denied despair

But charioted me aloft in this creation.

Aloft within,

*updesh (a dimension within a dimension)

Convent Covenant

Nineteen women in a white washed laundry,

Stiff white starched bonneted jailers

Chewing the cud on their rosaries,

Circumventing their promiscuous intention

To punish the joy jolly maidens,

For penetration of their maiden heads

On the white washed laundry.

13/2/13

Peter's Pence

Socratic images among Vatican gargoyles seemingly whispering.

Swiss wasp guards incline spear –image.

One-armed bandit tensed!

All the bells - Jackpot!

Troubled Vox Populi in St.Peter's Square, sensing possible deliverance.

Communist night-watchman in Coliseum opposite, giggling.

Il Padre sighs, remembers coercing childhood.

Could he now, surrender all?!

13/2/13

The Time

Ratzinger leaves the sinking ship.

Convention cardinals rush the gangplank,

Seeking Ambrosia settlements from the Holy See .

Peter's pence is at the helm,

An opportunity to share the realm

By linking arms with Buddhist, Moslem, and Hindu
brothers,

Where Krishna, Christ, Allah, and Buddha,

Might open wide Valhalla

13/2/13.

I am grateful for the help and invaluable support from: Rita, Brian, Pam, Anna, Curnán, Eugene, Mousa, John Colohan and especially Tony who was so patient with me in my tardy comprehension regarding publishing essentials. I also wish to thank members of: Kinvara Writers Group Co. Galway: Inis Writers Group, Ennis, Co. Clare: Three Legged Stool Poets, Ennis, Co. Clare: Linen Hall Writers, Castlebar, Co. Mayo: Westport Writers, Co. Mayo: for their friendship, encouragement, sensitivity and sacred good humour.

Donal O'Connell lives on an organic holding in Turlough, Bellharbour, in the heart of the Burren, a unique area in County Clare, Ireland.

Made in the USA
Charleston, SC
13 July 2013